Opening the Door to Freedom

with

Forgiveness Therapy

WAYNE KAUPPILA

CONTENTS

THE STORY OF ABE

Abe was four years old when the beatings started. His dad was young and the stress of early fatherhood coupled with the lack of effective parenting skills—along with the abuse that he had experienced as a child—led to his beating his own son. The beatings continued for eight years, and stopped only when his father was removed from his life. During the last six years of the beatings, Abe received counseling from many counselors. He had been hospitalized due to injuries suffered at the hands of his father, and Child Protective Services and school counselors had been involved from almost the beginning.

Abe's mother divorced his father and moved with her son to a new town. His mother remarried a peaceful man, but the effects of the abuse Abe suffered continued to show. Abe was often in fights at school. His grades hovered in the C-D range. Abe was troubled by recurrent fearful thoughts and feelings, and he had trouble sleeping. Violent nightmares interrupted his sleep and he would awake abruptly, dripping with sweat. He could not easily return to sleep for fear of the monster that awaited him in his dreams. His lack of sleep contributed to high anxiety levels.

Abe had a hard time expressing anger. Any expression of anger would connect him with his internalized anger towards his abuser, and he would explode. Medical doctors prescribed Ritalin to help him deal with his anger, but it didn't always work. He continued to get into fights at school.

In his mid-teens, Abe started to experiment with alcohol, with disastrous results. Every time he used alcohol, he got into trouble. Drinking didn't help with his anxiety level or his recurrent nightmares. His trouble with alcohol and anger led to a professional recommendation for anger management and alcohol awareness classes. There, he was told that he could control what goes on inside himself. The therapists gave instructions like, "Live in the present, not in the past" and "Try needlepoint to stay in the present!" These statements were useless to a teenage boy to help him deal with anger and anxiety issues. Abe was still waking up from his nightmares and related that his bed was often soaked with his sweat. He couldn't concentrate in school, in sports, or with his girlfriend. He had recurring thoughts like, "I need to stay busy all the time." To enjoy a moment's rest and be at peace was a luxury that Abe had never known. Despite his efforts, Abe's life was only getting worse.

At 19 years of age, Abe arrived at the counseling center for a lethality assessment, which is a predictive assessment of his potential danger to society. He had been involved in an assault and battery case where alcohol was involved. As Abe related his history, it became apparent that he was genuinely seeking for a solution to his problems. During previous counseling, Abe had attained a high awareness and acceptance of what had happened to him, but it didn't make the symptoms go away. A new type of therapy was described to Abe—the process of forgiveness—and was offered as a possible solution to his problems. The first step was to write a letter to his abuser to identify what had been done to Abe and how he felt about it. The next step was to write a prayer of forgiveness and repeat it daily until testing revealed that he had forgiven his abuser. After learning about the forgiveness therapy option, Abe wholeheartedly agreed that this might be the answer to his problems, and planned to start on the process in his next session.

Abe missed his therapy sessions for the next four weeks. Phone conversations and drop-in visits to reschedule indicated that he had started the process on his own. He had written a long letter to his father outlining how he had been abused and how he felt about it. Abe then wrote a prayer forgiving his dad for the abuse he had suffered, and said it daily.

During this time period, Abe's dad attempted to come back into his life. He contacted Abe and indicated that he wanted to meet. Abe was angry and afraid to face his abuser, but armed with his letter and a resolve to work through his issues, he agreed to the meeting. Abe met his dad and gave him the letter stating the abuse he had suffered and how he felt about it. Abe's dad read the letter, admitted to committing the abuse and apologized. Abe chose to forgive his dad for what he had done to him.

Abe returned to counseling after these events and related how much he had changed during the process of forgiving. He stated that he didn't have any more terrifying nightmares. He was sleeping through the night. His grades had climbed from Cs and Ds to As and Bs. His friends, parents, teachers and girlfriend have all noted positive improvements in Abe's daily functioning. His explosive anger has disappeared. The judge in his assault and battery case took note of all these positive changes. Abe feels much better about himself, and he is starting to establish a new relationship with his biological dad now that he has been freed from the bondage to a destructive past. Abe came to believe so much in the power of forgiveness that he wanted the process put down in writing so that he could use it to help his friends heal from similar circumstances—and so the idea for this book was born.

PREFACE

The wisdom found in this book is centuries old. It may even exist beyond the normal intellectual thought channels, and is, perhaps, knowledge contained in our genetic makeup. To tap into this genetic knowledge requires only honesty, openness, and willingness to experience the fullness of human possibility. That fullness can be viewed as health in mind, body, emotions, and spirit.

This book is about healing—healing from trauma, hurt and pain—that can block us from experiencing the fullness of our humanity. Scientists are beginning to study the biological differences between an angry, resentful person and a peaceful, forgiving person, and are finding physiological benefits from having a forgiving spirit.

But what happens when you can't forgive? When your spirit has been damaged, and you are blocked from even knowing it? When you look deep inside and all you find is resentment, hurt, and pain? When you're medicating your pain with alcohol or drugs or any of a myriad of addictive behaviors? Your insides are all chaos, and you lack purpose and direction in your life. There may be other problems, such as anxiety or depression, which result from holding in resentment, anger or pain.

Temporary solutions like drugs and alcohol often bring with them long-term problems and in the end are not worth it. Medications can also be used as a temporary solution and may be fully justified, but if the root problem is an unhealed trauma or resentment, working on healing this root cause may provide a deeper cure. It is often easier to find a diversion than to work on these traumas—and the world is full of diversions. Diversions and distractions can keep you from your truths—your pain and your power. A lifetime can be spent diverting oneself instead of finding true healing.

This book reminds us of the forgiveness solution. It's nothing new. We have the wisdom, but have forgotten how to use it.

The author was once told to forgive his mother for the harm she had done. He knew deep down inside that this was the key to his healing, but he didn't know how. This book is the result of his learning how to forgive and from observing the results of this healing knowledge being practiced with other trauma survivors.

The author has practiced the methods found in this book and has found healing. He has also helped clients, in his clinical practice, with these methods and has observed clinically significant improved functioning using Forgiveness Therapy.

You, too, are welcome into the fullness of the human race. Step through the door to freedom by opening this book and practicing the methods found within, and enjoy your new life.

This book presents a method to heal with forgiveness. It is a "how-to" book that answers the question, "How do I forgive?" Forgiveness Therapy was refined and practiced in a clinical setting, but the author believes that the forgiveness process can be used as a self-help method if the appropriate safeguards are taken. If you are going to try to help yourself with the methods in this book, please read Chapter 9 on safety precautions first.

The therapeutic process outlined in this book was developed over the course of several years. It was the author's own recovery from childhood abuse and alcoholism that provided the insight into the origins of this healing process. These insights came from several sources including counseling, peers, and visions. A Masters degree in Addiction Counseling from the Hazelden Graduate School of Addiction Studies provided an excellent education in the art and science of addiction counseling. Hazelden's history of joining the 12 Steps of AA with the science of psychology was instrumental in the author's acceptance of the struggles and tensions associated with joining the practices of spirituality and science.

This book also attempts to combine spirituality with the science of healing by delineating a series of clinical steps that show how to use the healing power of forgiveness. Admittedly, as a scientific endeavor, this therapy is only in its infancy, and relies solely on the faith of the author and the results so far obtained. It is the author's opinion that any new therapy arises not from a scientific study but from the beliefs of the founder, which then become validated by scientific study.

The philosophical underpinnings of this therapy are anchored in three areas. The first area is the universal spiritual principle of forgiveness. The second area is the 12 Steps of AA, which, when practiced for any length of time, lead to the acceptance that a life of sobriety is a life founded on spiritual principles. The third area is Person Centered Therapy, which maintains that in the center of every human being is a positive core. In the practice of Forgiveness Therapy, this positive core is seen to contain the knowledge of the concept of forgiveness, as evidenced by the fact that not one client lacked an understanding of what forgiveness is. Forgiveness Therapy becomes an extension of these areas by laying out clear therapeutic guidelines and procedures to heal by forgiving.

This therapeutic process of forgiveness was refined and practiced in an outpatient substance abuse treatment clinic and was offered as a path to healing for those clients who presented with a history of abuse. This abuse could be physical, mental, emotional or spiritual, but in many cases it was sexual in nature. Other forms of abuse that have been addressed by forgiveness therapy have been abandonment, neglect, broken first loves, children of alcoholics and addicts issues, racism, lack of love during childhood, marital affairs, religious abuse, poor parenting, death of a loved one, and different combinations of the above.

The process of forgiveness was developed, in part, using the story "Freedom From Bondage" from the book *Alcoholics Anonymous*, commonly referred to as the Big Book of AA (Alcoholic Anonymous World Services, Inc., 2001). The main idea of this story is to pray for the person toward whom you carry resentments. This idea was coupled with the universal spiritual principle of forgiveness, to take the idea one step further. The foundation of the therapy presented in this book is a prayer of forgiveness that the client composes and recites daily until testing reveals that they have resolved the issue. To be successful, the client is required to comprehend what it was they are trying to heal—their particular resentments.

In the population being treated at the clinic, resentments are often the major issue to be resolved if there is to be a possibility for long-term sobriety. This was known by the founder of AA, Bill W. He said, in *As Bill Sees It* (Alcoholics Anonymous World Services, Inc., 1967, page 39), "Resentment is the Number One offender. It destroys more alcoholics than anything else."

As the process evolved, it became evident that the first steps needed to include an assessment of the client's awareness, admittance and acceptance of the fact that they had suffered some type of abuse. Without these three prerequisites, clients remained in denial of what had actually happened to them. In fact, the failure to talk about what had happened to them—and their feelings associated with the events—was often viewed by the client as more significantly hurtful than the actual events. For example, one female client had suffered sexual abuse by a neighbor when she was a young girl, but when she told her dad, he didn't believe her. She told her mom, who confronted the neighbor's mother, who in turn said that it couldn't have happened. The incident was never spoken of again because the social facades of the participants took precedence over the girl's pain. In recalling her abuse, the girl had more resentment for her father than she had for her abuser. She also resented the socio-religious system that allowed and protected the continuance of this abuse. So, even though she had suffered sexual abuse, she needed to raise her awareness, admittance and acceptance that she had experienced other forms of abuse, and that this other abuse could be just as damaging, or even more damaging than the more obvious abuse.

These three prerequisites—awareness, admittance and acceptance—can be achieved by talk therapy and/or by the letter-writing exercise contained in this book. This part of the process can often be the most difficult portion of forgiving someone because it involves looking back at abuse issues, possibly for the first time. Some clients have had difficulty because this look back can be re-traumatizing, and some become suicidal in the process. For this reason, chapter 9 is devoted to safety. Safety issues are also behind the request that the process of forgiveness never be put forth as mandatory or required, but that it be offered freely as an option for healing. The client's freewill decision to forgive is a crucial aspect of the success of Forgiveness Therapy.

After a client demonstrated awareness, admittance, and acceptance, they were offered a letter-writing assignment to put in writing their feelings about the events that had happened. A loosely structured letter format was used that not only examined the negative feelings but also sought to find positive feelings from the past. The positive feeling part was omitted if the abuse was from a stranger, as in the case of rape by an unknown perpetrator. The letter-writing assignment was always accompanied by a feelings list, to help the client identify their feelings, and by emergency contact numbers for crisis lines and emergency rooms in case the process caused them to have suicidal ideas.

The next stage of the process is the prayer writing exercise. The client is asked if they are ready to write a prayer forgiving their abuser and if answered yes, the prayer format is quickly given to help resolve any fears the client may have about composing a prayer. The prayer format is found in Appendix 3. The client is directed to recite the prayer daily until testing determines they have forgiven their abuser.

The last stage in the process is forgiveness testing. The forgiveness test was developed to indicate the point when an issue is resolved. Simply asking the client if they were done with an issue didn't yield useful results because just asking the question allowed the client to remain in their defenses, which reside in the intellectual realm in their head. A method was needed to identify what a person was truly feeling. Erik Skarstrom, a classmate of the author at the Hazelden Graduate School of Addiction Studies, provided a method to help a person get in touch with their true emotions. The procedure he provided might be classified as a focusing technique, but wasn't presented as such. It is a procedure to identify the original feelings that a person is experiencing and takes the focus off any maladaptive thinking about one's feelings. It is also a spiritual practice that connects one to their heart. It is often said that the longest journey an alcoholic makes is the sixteen inches from their head to their heart, and this technique makes this journey much faster. The procedure is very simple and consists of putting one's dominant hand over their heart and speaking what they feel under their hand. This very powerful procedure takes people out of their defenses and connects them with their real feelings, which is especially useful when dealing with resentments that may have been harbored for numerous years, protected by many layers of defenses in the mind. The forgiveness test is to place one's dominant hand over the heart, close your eyes, make the statement "I forgive you (insert name of person)", and then identify the feeling under the hand. If the client identifies three positive or neutral feelings in succession, then the issue is considered resolved. If the client cannot identify a feeling, a feelings list, with the hand still on the heart, is used to help identify the feeling or resentment.

An outline of the steps of the process of Forgiveness Therapy is as follows: 1. Gain awareness of the abuse issues. 2. Gain admittance of having been abused. 3. Gain acceptance of having been abused. 4. Write a letter to identify the resentments. 5. Write a prayer of forgiveness and repeat daily. 6. Test if the issue is resolved.

This therapeutic process of forgiveness wasn't developed in any type of scientific environment. Each part was included as the need presented itself and as the solution to the need became apparent or available. There was no hypothesis and scientific study of the data; instead, there was a recognized need and a caring attitude that sought to find a method for healing. The parts of the solution arrived by several different paths and were synthesized into a working, effective therapeutic process that has been used to create fundamental positive change. As with any new therapy, the intuition of the therapist is the light in the darkness, which guides the development of the process. The therapy put forth in this book is in its infancy and has only been intuitively validated by the author and supported by the testimonies of the participants. The next obvious scientific step is to put the therapy through rigorous controlled studies to gain or refute scientific validation. But, the lack of scientific validation should not be a stumbling block to the use of this therapy by therapists or organizations who intuitively recognize the suitability of Forgiveness Therapy for the needs of their clients.

Forgiveness therapy can be viewed as a bridge between the science of psychology—an intellectual pursuit—and the spiritual realm of human experiencing. This spiritual realm can at first produce fear due to the very basic human proclivity to fear the unknown. Once this initial fear is conquered, the decision to build and walk over this bridge to better health can be made. An analogy of a bridge might help to see how these two areas can be linked. Picture these two areas—the scientific and the spiritual—as islands separated by an expanse of water with a bridge started from the science island. The initial building blocks are awareness, admittance and accepting. The bridge is further built with the letter-writing exercise, which identifies the wounds that need healing. The final building block is the freewill decision to forgive, which connects the bridge to the spiritual realm or island. On this island resides the power to heal.

The writer thanks his Higher Power for these gifts that have helped so many hurting people. I would like to thank my wife for supporting me through the development of this process. I also would like to express my gratitude to Erin for all her help on this book. I also give thanks to Erik Skarstrom and Kathleen P. for their valuable input. And to all my past clients, thank you for allowing me to be a part of your healing. Many of you have expressed a newfound sense of freedom that you have never known before. Your lives have changed dramatically and this book was written as a tribute to you. It was written to outline the process that helped you to change, and also that others may benefit from a process of forgiveness.

As required by Federal Law, all clients' identifying information has been removed or altered pursuant to 42CFR2 to protect the identities of the persons involved.

1

WHAT IS FORGIVENESS?

Forgiveness is a freewill, conscious decision to relieve someone of the debt that they believe another person owes them. It is also a decision to be spiritual, and to open oneself up to the spiritual powers inside of themselves. Just like a baby learning to walk, choosing a path of forgiveness involves learning to access your spiritual powers. You may have been hurt physically, mentally, emotionally, or spiritually by someone in your past. This injustice has left its impression on your heart and personality. In all probability, it is affecting your present-day relationships to an extent that you don't even know or comprehend. This negative energy has left its imprint on your heart. Forgiveness is a path to healing these wounds. Forgiveness allows one to be free from the bondage of one's past. Being free from the past allows us to live in the moment, without encumbrances.

Forgiveness is a conscious decision to pardon or grant a reprieve. When we think of granting a pardon or reprieve, it naturally follows that the person granting the pardon has some authority or power to relinquish the debt. This power or authority to forgive originates in the spiritual realm of human experiencing. This can be very empowering for victims of abuse. The intellect may reject this authority due to its tendency toward an "eye-for-an-eye" justice concept, but healing through forgiveness isn't in this realm.

There are four realms in which humans experience life: the physical, mental, emotional and spiritual. Past hurts or resentments may have been experienced in any of the four realms. Forgiveness is a spiritual solution for resentments. The power and authority to forgive is in the spiritual realm. The decision to forgive opens oneself up to the positive power available in this realm. The power to forgive is also the power that heals. It is the power to free oneself from past negative experiences. Opening up to the power in the spiritual realm creates new horizons in becoming fully human. This power is Love. Deciding to forgive, is loving yourself.

Why not Justice?

Clients often ask, "Why was I abused?" This question is in the mental/intellectual realm and indicates that the person is seeking for an answer in this realm. This question, "Why?" brings up the concept of justice. Justice exists in the mental realm, where a person is fully justified to hold on to past injustices. A person's anger and bitterness feels right — and is right when operating under ideas such as an "eye-for-an-eye." This kind of thinking, however, limits the human experience to just three realms — the physical, mental, and emotional. If the client restricts themselves to just these three realms, he restricts himself from the power to forgive and the healing available in the spiritual realm.

Justice is a strong concept that has a proper place in the mental, emotional and physical realms, but it isn't an avenue to use when seeking healing from past abuse. Clients are advised that staying with the justice concept will keep them stuck in the feelings of injustices that they have experienced. Their feelings of injustice are encouraged and validated, but where is there any healing power in this area? In the justice concept, or seeking for the "whys", there is little or no healing power.

If a client persists in searching for a solution by looking for an answer to the "whys", a metaphor is used to point out the insanity of abuse. The client is asked to imagine their abuse as a closed room that is completely darkened. They are asked to enter that room to find an understanding of their abuse. Understanding or sanity is portrayed as a light, even a very tiny light. If even this tiny bit of understanding or sanity were in the darkened room, it would light up the room. But there isn't any understanding or sanity in abuse. It is all insanity. It is all darkness. Trying to understand insanity is impossible by the very definition of the word "insane." All clients the author has worked with have abandoned looking for healing in the mental realm after this metaphorical discussion, which opens the possibility that their healing may be in the spiritual realm. This opens the door to a discussion about the nature of spirituality.

The difference between spirituality and religion is commonly misunderstood. Religion versus spirituality conflicts can be addressed by talking about universal spiritual concepts such as Love, charity, compassion and forgiveness, and then asking about the client's understanding of religion. Talking along these lines usually clarifies the difference between religion and spirituality. It is important to note that this process of forgiveness is a spiritual process and is not connected to any religion, or the converse that forgiveness is a universal spiritual concept found in most religions. Most religions seem to have forgiveness as one of their spiritual principles, but even if a person's religion doesn't contain forgiveness, the spiritual makeup of humanity seems to come endowed with some knowledge of forgiveness. The client can work with this knowledge without involving their religion, or the positive aspects of their religion that support the process of forgiveness can be utilized.

The Story of Jaba

Jaba's mother left when he was young. His drug-addicted dad abused him in almost any way a perverted mind could imagine. He suffered such torments as repeated rapes, beatings, starvation, and abandonment until the state took custody of him at age ten. By then, he believed he was totally hopeless. He followed almost exactly in his father's footsteps, even to the point of abusing his own children. Jaba was sent away for several years to the state penitentiary. While in prison, Jaba was befriended by a Voodoo practitioner who taught him the spiritual practices of the Voodoo belief system. When Jaba was released from prison, probation requirements brought him to the counseling center. There, he was offered a process of forgiveness to work on his resentments towards his father. Jaba said that Voodoo didn't have forgiveness as one of its principles, but that he knew what it was. He agreed to work the process with slight modifications in the wording of some methods. Jaba wanted to call it "granting his dad a reprieve" instead of forgiving. He also created a meditation for granting a reprieve instead of a prayer of forgiveness. With these changes, he worked through the process.

After granting his father a reprieve, Jaba realized significant improvements in his outlook on life. He began to focus on living instead of dying. He made plans and intends to go to college or technical school. He started new relationships that were grounded in honesty rather than fear. He was making attempts to repair or make amends to old hurtful relationships. Jaba even put forth real effort to try to find his dad and re-establish this relationship. Jaba wanted to see if he could help his dad to find healing.

Jaba related that, over the years, he had many types of counseling and therapy to try to help him to change, and all had done some good in his life. Jaba stated the he believes that going through the process of granting his father a reprieve was the best counseling he had ever received. He also stated that he sees the most positive change in himself and has more hope for his future now than ever before in his life.

Jaba had another experience that bears mentioning. It could be called an epiphany, moment of clarity, quantum change, or a transformational experience. Jaba had a vision—totally unexpected—where he could see his whole past with his father and how it had affected his life up to the granting a reprieve exercise. He could also see his present condition and experienced a sense of freedom for his future, which was full of hope and free of his past. His newfound freedom was experienced as a future with unlimited possibilities, unbound by his past abuse. He was exhilarated. His joy was evident many days after he had this experience, and he saw a direct correlation between granting his father a reprieve and his newfound freedom and joy. These types of experiences have happened to some people who have chosen to go through this process, and a chapter is devoted to the subject further on in this book.

Jaba's story demonstrates many of the qualities of the forgiveness process. It demonstrates the human capacity to know what forgiveness is regardless of the wording. Jaba granted a reprieve to his dad for many years of abuse—the same spiritual concept as forgiveness. The other concepts in Jaba's story will be discussed in following chapters.

The Importance of a Freewill Decision.

In all cases presented in this book, a process of forgiveness was offered as a possible path to healing. The clients were free to choose other therapies, such as Rational Emotive, Cognitive Behavioral, or Twelve Step Facilitation. In a majority of the cases in this book, the clients had already been through several treatments for substance abuse, mental health, anger management, or mental health counseling, and were open to trying something different because they were, as the saying goes, "sick and tired of being sick and tired." Most clients had also served or were facing jail or prison time and so had extra motivation to try anything to keep them from making the same mistakes again. The decision to participate was still offered as a free choice. Because the decision to forgive an abuser is an intensely personal matter, forcing a client to participate in a process of forgiveness was never considered an option, because it would be another form of abuse and therefore an unethical action. The abused population appears to be highly sensitive to hypocrisy, probably because of the abuse by people who were expected to love and care for them. Abusing them further by forcing them to try to forgive past abusers would have been hypocritical and unproductive. If a client chose not to participate in a process of forgiveness, that decision was respected. This freewill decision was also continued during the process, and if a client wanted to stop or slow down or even end the process, their decision was respected.

The client's freewill decision to forgive also results in a power gain. There is the obvious empowerment from the client choosing his or her own therapy, and the less obvious power gain that happens when a client chooses a spiritual path to healing. Some clients could also see how they would be more powerful than their abuser if they forgave the abuser. At first, this spiritual path may generate fear because it is unfamiliar, and it is here that the clinician's belief in the process lends power to the client trying it for the first time. Some clients, such as Abe, saw this spiritual power and ran with it on its own inertia. Other clients weren't as sure and tried the process out on small resentments until they learned to trust it, and then went on to larger resentments. The options were always their free choice.

Two Types of Forgiveness

There are two types of forgiveness for interpersonal relationships. The first type is forgiveness for wrongs that one has committed and for the ensuing guilt. It is forgiveness for an injustice committed against another human being, when we want some resolve for the guilty feelings arising from our actions.

The second type of forgiveness is forgiving someone who has hurt us but won't admit to it even if confronted. It can be forgiving past hurts arising from powerless situations, such as the abuse of children. It can be forgiving people who have died or have left in some other way. It is forgiveness where there is only one person participating in the process. The abuser need not participate and is, in fact, kept out of the process.

This book was written for the second type of forgiveness situation. It was written to help people to be free from past abuse, to help people live fuller lives.

Forgive and Forget?

People going through this therapy often ask if they should forgive and forget. The answer is no; the appropriate response is to forgive and learn from the experience. This is amplified in cases where there is the possibility of further abuse. It would be unsafe to have a victim forgive an abuser and forget about it, only to put the victim in a situation where more abuse is possible. In some cases, victims may be emotionally blocked from taking action against an abuser. Forgiveness removes the emotional blocks so that positive action can take place.

Another area where "forgive and forget" often comes up is with broken loves or infidelity. Clients with these types of resentments often want to forgive by forgetting, but they are reminded that if they don't learn from the experience, they are more likely to repeat it.

Forgetting can be viewed as wanting to go back to a time of innocence, a contracting of the human experience. Forgiving is an expansion of the human experience, so the saying "forgive and forget" seems to be a self-contradicting statement. "Forgive and learn" is a more appropriate replacement.

2

AWARENESS

The Story of Daisy

Daisy, a female in her mid-twenties, came to the counseling center under court order due to alcohol related charges. She attended counseling for several months but continually relapsed. It became increasingly apparent that there might be some deeper issues that were being missed in treatment. A re-assessment found that her father had died of a self-inflicted gunshot when she was young. Some time later, her mother remarried an emotionally and physically abusive man, and Daisy witnessed the physical beatings of her mother. Daisy herself had been the victim of verbal and emotional abuse. She had tried to excel in academics to gain some validation by her step dad, but the message was always the same: "You made this mistake, you made that mistake, couldn't you have done better?" Daisy wasn't allowed to express any emotion at home or her step dad would say, "Children are to be seen, not heard." This continued through her high school years.

Daisy turned to alcohol and marijuana as a refuge, finding acceptance among her friends who drank and smoked weed. She tried to forget her past and moved out of her parents' house at age 17, determined to make it on her own. She failed miserably. Broken relationships, sporadic employment and increasing drug and alcohol abuse landed her in jail many times.

Throughout her first months of counseling, Daisy presented a proud and perfect facade. Then, an incident happened where she experienced uncontrollable rage towards a male who was close to her. To cope, she turned to alcohol and again landed in jail. This incident, along with the re-assessment, indicated that Daisy had a secret cache of anger that even she wasn't aware of. She had never presented any anger prior to this incident, even stating, "I am not an angry person." Her perfectionism prevented the expression of any real anger. She could put on a show of anger to control and manipulate, but real expression of anger was foreign to her.

Through counseling, Daisy was able to begin to look at how she was abused as a child. She confronted her stepfather, even though advised not to, and he reacted by stating that none of it happened and that she was "just being a bitch." In doing so, he put her in the same emotional place she had been so often as a child.

Daisy tried to get in touch with the anger she felt towards her biological father by writing a letter to him, but wasn't very successful. Next, she wrote a letter to God expressing her anger towards Him for taking her dad and realized that it was really her father she was mad at for being so selfish as to take his own life.

Daisy chose to write prayers of forgiveness to her stepfather, biological father, and God. She chose forgiveness as a path of healing. Daisy's process is a slow one, and she is still working on it.

Daisy's story brings to light that awareness of what needs forgiving isn't always obvious at first inspection. The core issues that could be healed by forgiveness may be obscured by perfectionism, fear, alcoholism or drug addiction, denial, pride, or by a whole host of other maladaptive coping mechanisms that a person may have developed or acquired to help them to feel good about themselves.

A common, and very damaging, concealment factor of abuse is family denial. Family denial is a multi-layer system of denial of abuse. At the very core, the person experiencing the abuse is given the message that their experience, the abuse, wasn't real or didn't happen, that the way they perceived the event wasn't accurate or that their feelings aren't right. They may be told the abuse never happened, couldn't have happened, or didn't happen that way. This denial blocks the awareness of what kind of abuse happened or even if it did happen.

Another level of denial is that the victim isn't allowed to process the abuse event. They aren't allowed to talk about it or express their feelings connected with the event. This message can come from several different social levels.

The larger the social grouping that participates in the denial, the greater the layers of denial. For example, if in a cultural grouping of people, physical punishment routinely exceeds the limit of punishment and enters into abuse, there will probably exist several layers of denial that need to be worked through to expose the abuse for what it is. The outermost layer is cultural acceptance by the group. A victim willing to gain awareness of their abuse is risking rejection by their own culture. The cultural message may be that "we don't talk about such things." After penetrating this cultural level, deeper and more powerful level of denial would then be exposed—the family denial discussed earlier.

The last and most powerful level of denial for people abused by their own parents can be summed up in the statement, "How could my parent(s), who are supposed to love and care for me, abuse me?" This level of denial is extremely strong due to the message that parental abuse carries: that the abused is worthless. The feeling of worthlessness is similar to feeling non-existent, and non-existence needs to be denied by the very person who feels it. A person's perceived value in life originates in the value placed on the infant/child by the parental figures. If there is no valuing, the child feels no value. Parental abuse, in its many forms, and differing in magnitude, conveys that message that the child is worthless, valueless. This form of denial appears to be the most challenging layer to work through in exposing abuse issues and raising awareness. This is because the person is stepping out of the abused child role, thereby giving up the fantasies of ideal parents who should have loved them perfectly, and stepping in the role of a more responsible adult who is willing to take responsibility for their own healing. There is a type of double whammy effect here: first, the adult/child is giving up its idealized vision of its parents, and second, they are gaining awareness that not only didn't the parents not love the child perfectly, but abused them as well. Forgiveness becomes a catalyst at this very crucial point of change due to the fact that the client can see that through forgiveness there is the possibility of a new, more mature type of relationship with the parental figures. Without forgiveness, a person standing at this double whammy point usually sees breaking off the relationship as the only option.

Some clients presented with a high level of awareness of their abuse issues. One such client was Abe, who had achieved increased awareness due to extensive prior counseling. Awareness of the abuse issues can be gained through normal therapeutic methods, which can identify and work through the layers of defenses that guard the core issues.

Awareness of other abuse issues needs to be a continuing part of forgiveness therapy due to the intimate and deep nature of the work. When a client opens up to forgiving past resentments, they are sometimes opening their consciousness to other areas that they don't know exist. In these unknown subconscious areas might reside other abuse issues and the alert clinician keeps an open ear to them.

Awareness of other resentments seems to be fairly obvious — marital affairs, death, broken loves, rape, and other forms of sexual abuse. There is another form of abuse that has taken quite a bit of talking in order to raise the awareness level, and that is abuse by a larger system, such as a culture, organization, government, etc. Clients who have been raised in abusive cultures don't usually recognize the fact, but when the abusive cultural influences are pointed out, they can see the abuse and its effects on them. Some clients have chosen to forgive whole cultures, but the effectiveness of this method is hard to gauge due to the existential nature of the problem.

A method to help gain awareness is the time line. The time line is simply a line drawn on paper, which is divided up into the years of a person's life. The events are placed in their respective years. To start the time line, put down an event that is easily remembered and then work chronologically, either backwards or forwards, into the areas where memory may be lacking. This seems to trigger the remembrance of events that are blocked. Other therapeutic methods that cause regression can also be used to help identify resentments.

Awareness of past resentments can be likened to a metaphor of being bound. Harboring one, strong resentment, it is like being bound up with one large, strong rope. Harboring several resentments is like being bound by several medium strength ropes and harboring many resentments is like being bound by many threads. In all three of these situations, the person is bound from living life freely. Forgiveness therapy is an effective method to breaking all of these bonds.

Abuse can be very subtle or it can be very blatant. How does a person, especially a child raised in an abusive home, know what abuse is? A simple answer to this question is to answer the question "Do (or did) I feel loved and cared for?" If the answer is "No", then there is a good possibility that abuse happened or is happening. This question can be asked for one incident or for a span of time. For example: a young girl is raped, but mom and dad refuse to accept her story and won't validate her emotions associated with the rape. The little girl could ask, "Do I feel loved and cared for by my parents in this situation?" The obvious answer of "No" indicates that her parents are abusing her in addition to the abuse she has already suffered. For children reading this book: if you were to ask yourself this question, "Do I feel loved and cared for?" and the answer is no, then you need to look for people who will listen and care about what you have to say.

Feelings are the human indicator of the status of life. Listening to one's feelings and talking to someone who cares about them is an excellent way to raise awareness of resentments or abuse. Feelings lists are used extensively throughout this process to gain and maintain awareness of what is being worked on. Looking at resentments can often be a very painful process and the appropriate use of feelings lists makes it somewhat easier. In almost every session, clients are given a feelings list and asked to circle the feelings that they are experiencing. This gives the clinician a good indicator of their progress. Feeling lists are also used in the letter-writing exercise and in the forgiveness testing portions. The use of feelings lists raises the awareness of not only the resentment or abuse, but also of the good feelings that happen when healing occurs.

3

ADMITTING

Once awareness of resentments has been achieved, the next step in the process is to admit that there is a problem that needs to be worked on. Some clients have taken a stance that certain forms of physical abuse were "just what everybody did back in the day." They use this rationalization to deny their feelings associated with the physical abuse. This is where the use of a feelings list is useful to help clients to see that they are still re-feeling the past and that these re-feelings, these resentments, are what need to be worked on. This situation can be complicated by judgmentalism, where the client doesn't want to look at abuse issues, especially by parents, because they feel that they are then judging their parents as totally bad. It is here that a discussion about right and wrong is appropriate, saying that there is no right or wrong in the counseling process, everything just is. The judgmental client often makes generalizations about the rightness or wrongness of their abusers, but it can be pointed out that all people make mistakes. This seems to help clients who don't want to "leave" their parents or demonize them in this process. This emotional separation from parental abusers appears to be difficult due to the double whammy effect discussed in the last chapter. This emotional separation has been made less difficult if the client has first admitted to emotional immaturity and has done some work on identifying and expressing their emotions.

Admitting to abuse can lead to the breakdown of internalized family and cultural structure and leave the client uncertain about their place in the family or culture. It can be an extreme internal upheaval for even a grown person to admit and say for the first time something like "I didn't feel loved by my mom," or, "my dad raped me." The whole internal idealized structure can fall apart, which can lead to identity crisis and also more serious problems. For that reason, there is a chapter devoted to safety further along in this book. Anyone reading this book and trying to work this process on their own is urged to read the chapter on safety before proceeding through the process.

It is one thing to look at abuse on an intellectual level, but it is a much more emotionally loaded event to look at and admit to the feelings of being abused. Yet, it is these very feelings that cause the negative effects. These traumatic feelings are the fibrous ropes that keep us bound to the past, kept from experiencing a full and free life.

Another matter that often comes up with admitting to abuse is that clients question whether or not they need to confront the abuser. The answer is always no. This answer needs to be qualified with the following statements: the clinician is a mandatory reporter of child abuse situations, and that if the law was broken, the appropriate authorities will be contacted. Clients who have gone ahead and confronted their abusers, against advice, have had mixed results. Abe got excellent results. His dad confessed to the abuse and had a repentant spirit. Daisy, on the opposite extreme, got more abuse when she tried to confront her stepfather, and this confrontation has made it extremely hard for her to move forward in forgiving him. In many cases it appears that the abuser will deny the abuse ever happened, and so it is recommended that the client not confront the abuser. It is left open to the client that if in the future, when they have more emotional maturity, they might want to confront the abuser but be prepared for more abuse or denial. Additionally, the client is warned to be on the lookout for family support of the denial.

An emotion that is often encountered in working with abuse issues is anger. The abused person will often express anger as a defense to looking at their abuse. This anger needs to be validated, as it is righteous anger. They have a right to be angry. If a client has a difficult time processing or admitting to their anger, a good way for them to see it is to put it in a third party scenario. For example, lets say a client was raped as a child, but can't admit to her anger about the event. A third party scenario would be to have the client imagine that she was witness to the rape of a child and then ask what she felt about it. The client would probably express anger and then the question would be posed that, "Why don't you feel that same anger about your own situation?" This method has helped rape victims get in touch with their own anger about their abuse and begins to touch on the deeper emotions of the abuse. Underneath the anger are usually tears. These unshed tears may have been there for decades but still need to come out. These emotions are the resentments that forgiveness can heal.

The Story of Cameo

Cameo was a female in her young twenties. Her life had been steadily getting worse. She got her third DUI, which brought her into court-mandated counseling. Cameo was open about her past history including her sexual molestation by a relative when she was ten years old. She said that the abuse had been successfully addressed because she had received some counseling shortly after it happened. Cameo's difficulty was in expressing her emotions. She couldn't figure out what she was feeling even about the smallest events. Her emotions seemed to be frozen. Cameo could talk about events at the physical or intellectual level, but there were no emotions. A metaphor was used with Cameo to help her to see where the emotions might be frozen. The metaphor was that the sexual molestation event had created a frozen soap bubble about the size of a bowling ball, and that she was holding on to this frozen bubble with both hands to keep it from shattering. The bubble she was protecting was the frozen emotions of the abuse. The bigger problem was that all of her emotional energy was being used to keep the frozen bubble from shattering. She agreed that this is what it was like, that all her emotions were frozen and she was maintaining them in this fashion because she didn't know what else to do. The problem was that life was creating more and more emotions that wouldn't stay frozen and she didn't know how to deal with them, so she would drink and smoke pot in an attempt to cope. Cameo was asked what she would like to do with the frozen soap bubble she was carrying around. She said that she would like to have it melt and then wash her hands of it. We used the aforementioned method of third partying the abuse event and Cameo was able to express anger towards her abuser for the first time. After we got through with the anger, she released the tears that hadn't been cried in almost a decade. Cameo had stated earlier that "I never cry," but now the tears flowed freely as she talked about how much she had been hurt by her molester. Cameo was admitting to and expressing those frozen emotions that she had been carrying around for years.

It took some time for Cameo to admit to and accept her emotions about this abuse event. After about a month of emotion work, Cameo was ready to forgive her abuser. She wrote a prayer of forgiveness and said it daily for another month, until testing revealed that she had, in fact, forgiven her abuser.

Some of the benefits that Cameo realized from her forgiving her abuser were an awareness and ability to express her emotions, higher self-esteem, the ability to establish and maintain boundaries, and the ability to quickly resolve disputes with other family members. Her drug and alcohol use diminished to no use at all. When asked about the soap bubble towards the end of her process, she said that it is melted and gone, leaving only a few small color stains on her hands.

On an intellectual level, Cameo could admit to the abuse that had happened to her, but on an emotional level she couldn't even identify the associated emotions. It took some time for her to admit to the resentments that were causing her so much trouble. The effects of this sexual molestation were, in a large part, the causative factors of Cameo's drug and alcohol addiction and to her three DUIs.

The admittance that is needed for this process is an admittance of the feelings or emotions that are binding us to the past. An intellectual or just a physical recounting of the event doesn't identify the resentments. These resentments will probably be buried by defenses that have been developed or acquired to protect the vulnerable feelings.

Clients need to see in their therapist the ability to go with them into their vulnerable feelings associated with abuse issues and to help them find a way to heal these resentments. What would be the use of opening up this area of feelings, which is basically re-traumatizing the client, if one didn't possess the tools to help heal? Forgiveness therapy is a powerful tool to help clients heal from past abuse or resentments.

4

ACCEPTING

The Story of Ted

Ted was beaten repeatedly by his mother until he was eight. At that tender age he had to stand up to his mother and fight back in an act of adult aggression that he had learned from his parents' many fights. Ted's mother then manipulated his father into taking over the beatings and they continued until Ted was twelve. For some reason, still a mystery, the beatings stopped. The damage didn't stop. The emotional scars that Ted carried affected him daily. He couldn't keep a job for more than two or three months. Ted had gotten married at a young age, and the couple had several children. This didn't settle Ted, and he continued to change jobs frequently. As the stress of supporting a family became greater, Ted needed to find a way to handle it and turned to alcohol. Several years of drinking did nothing to improve Ted's situation, and eventually Ted's wife gave him the ultimatum: quit drinking or get divorced. Ted entered counseling for alcoholism but soon found out that he had other problems. The issue of childhood abuse became a recurrent theme in his treatment plans. Ted had always joked about the "spankings" he had received stating that if he "didn't get one every other day something must be wrong." Ted used excuses like "everybody beat their children back then," or, "it was expected."

Through counseling, Ted raised his awareness of his abuse and how it was affecting his current functioning—Ted himself abused his own children. A confrontation with his parents did nothing to help the situation because they denied it ever happened and tried to shame him into conforming to the family rules. In other words, "Shame on you, we don't talk about such things." Ted struggled with accepting that what had happened to him was, in fact, abuse. To accept it as abuse meant that he had to give up his place in his family of origin. He had to go against the unspoken family and cultural rules of not talking about problems, and in the end he had to forego his part of the family inheritance in order to move forward with the healing process. Accepting the fact that he was abused was difficult for Ted because he had to give up his idealized fantasy about having perfect parents. He also had to admit and accept that the parents who should have loved and cared for him perfectly, didn't, and also, that they abused him. Ted's acceptance was also complicated by the fact that the abusers, his parents, didn't admit to any abuse. Ted's larger socio-religious community also rejected him because of his quest for healing.

Through many years of counseling, Ted raised his awareness of his abuse, admitted to being abused, and accepted that it had happened to him; but he still had resentments. A letter-writing exercise indicated that he still held resentments towards his mother, and he couldn't remember anything loving that she had ever done for him. Finally, Ted tried to forgive his mother. He said his prayer and asked God to forgive her as well. Subsequent forgiveness testing revealed that Ted had forgiven his mother. He is now expressing a new joy for life, free from alcohol and the bondage to his abusive past. He is also starting to remember some of the loving things his mother had done for him as a child.

The above case illustrates the next step on the journey of forgiveness—acceptance of the injustice done to a person. Acceptance is a further breakdown of the denial, which has protected the vulnerabilities damaged by the abuse. It is a cold hard look at the realities of what happened and the resulting emotional scars. Acceptance is in no way an approval of abuse, but is an honest look back into the past with the hope that healing can lead to a better future. That hope is found in forgiveness therapy.

Acceptance is about living life on life's terms, and this can be rough. Asking someone with low self-esteem to look at their abuse can be an extremely difficult thing to do. Clients who have been working through this process have become suicidal. (See the Chapter 9 on Safety.) This is due to the emotions of hopelessness, helplessness and worthlessness that are dredged up during this process. A child enduring abuse has these feelings but is at a loss to identify or express them. When looking back on these issues as an adult, the feelings are re-felt with a greater awareness of what they are. Consequently, the magnitude and severity of the feelings of hopelessness, helplessness and worthlessness can bring a person to consider suicide as an option, but hopefully not the only option. This is where the therapist's or the client's belief in the healing power of forgiveness can be the open door to another option, an option for a life free from the bondage of past abuse issues.

It is at the point of accepting where the freewill decision to forgive appears to be made. The decision to either forgive and live a free life, or to not forgive and continue to live life in bondage, perhaps regressing even to the point of suicide. Substance abuse increase has been noted as a part of this regression.

Accepting is a process and therefore takes time. The level of acceptance is also a factor and is dependent on the intensity of the abuse. Clients can often talk about the physical facts of the abuse or event. Some can make rationalizations about the cause and effects that may be involved, such as, "She cheated on me because I was always at the bar." But mostly, accepting is an honest look at the emotional damage done. It is looking into oneself for the emotional scars that need healing.

Men and women seem to approach accepting differently. Men tend to want to "get it done" as fast as possible and thereby expose themselves to a more intense emotional experience. Women seem to approach acceptance in a more piecemeal fashion. They seem to be self-regulating of the emotional intensity that they are willing to expose themselves to. Women appear to have an innate timing as to what to work on and when, so that they don't experience too much emotional intensity. Women are still given the same precautions as men and these precautions are discussed in the chapter on safety.

Each stage of the forgiveness process seems to have certain emotions associated with it. The awareness stage is marked by a lack of emotions, mostly due to the intellectual nature of educating on what is abuse and resentment. People in the admitting stage often have anger as their primary emotion, which is right and needed as previously discussed. The acceptance stage is often marked by resignation and a determination to heal. The wise clinician can determine what stage the client is in and work forward from that point. Some clients, who have had much counseling, present with a high awareness, admittance and acceptance of their abuse issues and need only an explanation of what a resentment is and how it can affect current functioning. Most of these clients are then ready to try forgiveness as a path to healing. Other clients present with no awareness of their abuse issues and so need to spend time in raising awareness, admittance and acceptance before the resentments can be worked on. Clients will indicate what issues they are willing to work on and how fast they want to work on them. The compassionate therapist can always ask, "Are you ready to work on this issue?" If the answer is no, then let it go for another session, because the freewill decision to forgive is essential to this therapy. This process has never been forced on a client because it would appear to be hypocritical to force someone to forgive. It probably wouldn't work and may in fact have negative consequences for the client.

If a clinician chooses to use forgiveness therapy with a client, it seems appropriate to make an assessment of the client's comprehension of awareness, admittance and acceptance of their abuse/resentment issues, so that the client gets a clear picture of the problem and also of the improvements that might be expected from healing. The letter-writing exercise, explained in the next chapter, can then be used to identify the resentments that need healing.

5

LETTER WRITING

Writing a letter to the person who caused the resentments is a method of documenting the feelings at the root of the client's troubles. The letter-writing assignment is combined with feelings lists (see Appendix 4) to aid in the identification of those feelings that keep one in bondage to the past. Emergency numbers are always included on the letter format (See letter format in Appendix 1).

Most clients' first question is, "Will the letter be sent?" and the answer is always no. The letter is being written to identify the resentments, not to confront the abuser. Clients are advised that in the future they may want to send the letter to confront their abusers, but this would only be done once the client has processed the resentment and gained a measure of emotional healing. This is recommended because most abusers, when confronted, will deny the abuse ever happened, thereby furthering the abuse. A client needs emotional strength to deal with such a situation. The risk here is that if the abuse happened when the client was young, it is very easy to regress to childhood behaviors when the abuser tries to deny, control or manipulate.

The letter-writing format used is as follows:

Emergency Numbers_____

Dear (insert name), This is what you gave me that I am thankful for...

This is what you did to me, and this is how I feel....

This letter format is given out in a printed form (see Appendix 1). It is always given with a feelings list (see Appendix 4) to help the client identify those feelings that they may have never known to be associated with the abuse.

The first part of the letter is for situations where there might be some positive feelings from the relationship—if a parent isn't perceived as all bad and the client can remember some good things about their parent. This helps the client to start to gain a more balanced view of the person. If the client can't remember anything good from a relationship, as in the case of rape by a stranger, then the first part of the letter can be omitted.

Putting the feelings/resentments down on paper has an extra therapeutic benefit in that it relieves some of the negative internal emotional energy that the client carries. If clients can't write the emotions down, they are recommended to just circle them on the feelings list.

An alternate line that can be used in the second line of the letter is, "This is what you didn't give me and this is how I feel." This would be appropriate for situations where one didn't receive the love, caring, respect etc., that was needed. The story of Grace demonstrates the use of both lines.

The Story of Grace

Grace had a difficult childhood. Her mother, a prostitute, had abandoned her at the age of three. She had lived with aunts, uncles and grandparents. The living conditions were not good—she was often neglected and was raped by her grandfather and by an uncle. Her father, a drug addict, couldn't care for her either, and when she went to stay with him, he let her know that he didn't care for her. Grace became a tough child of the streets. She wouldn't let anybody hurt her, which lead to several assault and battery convictions.

When Grace entered court ordered counseling at age 17, she was as tough as nails. Grace conformed her way through the court ordered counseling; she knew how to work the system. She would attend all sessions and say the right things so that she would be completed and discharged from counseling.

A few months later Grace contacted the counseling center and indicated that she wanted to restart counseling. She never did state what had been her motivation, but there were indications that her drug use was getting out of control. It was different this time around; Grace wanted to talk. She spoke, for the first time about her history of sexual abuse and that she had been raped several times by family members. She said that the legal system knew about these rapes and the perpetrators had been prosecuted, but that the schools, the foster care system and the counselors knew nothing of these rapes. These institutions saw her as a drug addicted child with an anger problem.

Grace was offered forgiveness as a path to healing her resentments, and she chose to give it a try. She agreed to start by working on a less severe issue first and wrote a letter to her neglectful father. She used the format line of "This is what you didn't give me, and this is how I feel." She identified resentments of feeling unloved, abandoned, and worthless. She wrote that her father would spend his money on drugs instead of on her needs. He would abandon her for some new girlfriend. He would show some care for his other children and none for Grace. Grace wrote a prayer of forgiveness to her father and repeated it several times per day. She said that she often repeated it at night when her fear and anxiety were preventing her from sleeping. She said that saying the prayer helped her to sleep. Grace continued to say this prayer for about one month, until testing revealed that she had forgiven her dad. This process prompted Grace to initiate her own letter-writing to her mother. She was gaining trust in the process of forgiveness. Forgiving her mom took much less time than it had taken to forgive her father, even though her issues with mom were more severe.

Grace was getting more in touch with her emotions. She could cry. She cried about the hurt from the rape by her grandpa, uncle and another adult male. She wrote letters to them using the format line, "This is what you did to me, and this is how I feel." Grace now trusted her ability to forgive, aided by the forgiveness process, to effectively free her from these past bondages. Grace was able, in one session, to write the letter identifying the resentments and also write a prayer forgiving the abuser. By the next week she would test as being finished with the issue.

One might suspect that Grace knew the expectations of the counselor and was giving the expected responses, but evidence to the contrary was numerous and powerful. Grace related that she was identifying other people who had hurt her, and she was working on forgiving them outside of the counseling relationship. Other evidence of positive change was that she wasn't getting into trouble in school and her grades were rising. Grace came into a group session in tears; she had a black eye and her nose was swollen. When asked what had happened, Grace related that a classmate had accused her of "narcing" on her drug use and had assaulted her in the school hallway. Grace stated that she didn't hit back. Remember that Grace had several previous assault and battery convictions. She took a battering from this girl without reciprocating. When Grace was asked why she didn't hit back, she replied, "I've changed. I'm now a child of God."

Grace's story demonstrates how both letter formats can be used in the therapeutic process. It demonstrates how working on less severe issues first builds trust in the process so that when the time comes to work on more severe issues, the client trusts in and has faith in the forgiveness process to heal past wounds. Grace also demonstrated how the process could be extended outside of the counseling setting to work on other resentments or abuse issues. The process can trigger the remembrance of other troublesome issues. Grace had never spoken of abuse or neglect by her mom, but in writing the letter to her dad she started to remember abuse and neglect by mom that was more severe than the abuse from her dad. Grace showed us that the process, due to its simplicity, could be used by people without the help of trained counselors or therapists. She did the work on her mother issues on her own with only the forgiveness testing done by her therapist. It is important to note that if one is to attempt this on their own, they need to know that they could become suicidal. Appropriate contacts need to be made readily available if this happens.

Timing is another important point of Grace's story. It took Grace several weeks to work through forgiving her dad, but only one week to forgive a rapist. Three factors are at work here. First is the allowance of time to become familiar and trust the healing process. Second is the duration of the abuse, which correlates to the amount of resentments. In Grace's case there was long term, continuous abuse and neglect by her father. The third factor affecting timing, and one that should be minimized, is the counselor's perception of the severity or intensity of the abuse. It is not up to the counselor to determine the relative importance of the issues. This is best left up to the client.

These three complicating factors, and probably many more, affect how much time a client will spend on each issue. The important thing to remember is to let the client determine how much time they need to spend with each issue and be careful not to force them into some predetermined schedule. Test to see if they are finished with each resentment and ask if they are ready to move on to the next issue. Some clients have taken months just to write the letter to an abuser, and never did want to forgive. Others have learned how to work the process on their own and have gone out and done their own work on their own time. And some clients work on forgiving at varying speeds, depending on the issue. Kaspar presented just such a variance in the time he took to work through his resentments.

The Story of Kaspar

Kaspar was a middle aged man. He had lost a good job from complications arising, in part, from his use of alcohol and drugs. He was also having trouble staying in a relationship for any length of time. Kaspar also had some severe mental health issues that were not being taken care of and were getting worse because of his drug and alcohol use. When Kaspar entered counseling he was suicidal. Mental health counseling and medication, along with substance abuse counseling, stabilized Kaspar's symptoms, and he was now ready to work on his resentments. Forgiveness therapy was not started or even talked about until Kaspar was stabilized.

Kaspar had three resentments that he could identify. Two were sexual abuse incidents from his late teens and early twenties, and the third was a neglectful father. Kaspar chose to work on the less severe of the sexual abuse events first. He wrote the letter identifying the resentments and wrote a prayer forgiving this abuser. Testing revealed that he was finished with this resentment. Next, Kaspar chose to work on the second abuse incident, which was sexual abuse by a male. Kaspar struggled for weeks to write the letter to this abuser. When asked if he wanted to even work on this issue, he stated that yes, he wanted to be done with it, but that it was hard work admitting to the intensity of the feelings he had about this abuser. At one point he said that he felt like he would kill him, if he only knew where to find him. Kaspar eventually did write the letter identifying his resentments towards this abuser. Later, he happened to be in the town where the abuse had taken place, and he felt no urge to go and hurt his abuser. It was postulated that perhaps Kaspar had forgiven his abuser without ever having written the prayer of forgiveness. Kaspar agreed to a forgiveness test to see if this was so, and it was. Kaspar had forgiven this abuser and harbored no more resentments towards him. Kaspar then wanted to move on to the resentments he had towards his father. He wrote a three-page letter describing how his father hadn't been there for him when he was growing up, even though they lived in the same house. His father had provided the basics of food and shelter, but never attended any of Kaspar's sporting events. He had never shown any interest in Kaspar's life or in his struggles while growing up. Dad would give all his attention and caring toward whatever girlfriend he had at the time, and none to Kaspar.

Kaspar was never able to write a prayer of forgiveness to his father. Their relationship hasn't changed—it is still distant and cold. Kaspar is still in bondage to the childhood dynamics in his relationship with his father, but other areas of Kaspar's life have changed for the better. He got a good job and his life improved dramatically. Kaspar is in a new, growing relationship and isn't using drugs or alcohol to cope with problems. He has hope and plans for his future. All suicidal ideation and plans have vanished. Kaspar indicated that he wasn't ready to forgive his dad even though he has seen the benefits of forgiving others who have hurt him. It is up to Kaspar to decide when he is ready to heal his wounds from his father. When the time comes, he knows how.

The timing of when to forgive is totally up to the client. They decide when and who to forgive and also who they won't forgive. Why would Kaspar forgive his abusers and not his father? The whys cannot be answered, because it is not an intellectual process. Rather, it is a spiritual process and needs to be accepted as such. It is up to Kaspar to forgive his dad when he chooses.

6

A PRAYER OF FORGIVENESS

The next step in this process of forgiveness is the prayer-writing exercise. The prayer is composed starting with the simple format. (Also, see Appendix 3 for the prayer format.)

Emergency Numbers_____

(Insert name of abuser), I forgive you for (then list three or four of the most significant resentments from the letter-writing exercise).

If the client has a belief in a Higher Power, for example God, then it is recommended that the next statement be included in the prayer:

I ask God to forgive you also.

Use whatever name they use for their Higher Power. So a prayer by a person who has been abandoned and hurt by their father might say: "Dad, I forgive you for the hurt and abandonment. I ask God to forgive you also."

It is recommended that the prayer be said at least once per day. It is recommended that the prayer be kept short and not too long in listing all of the resentments identified in the letter. Another point is to list the feelings (the resentments) and not the physical events. For example, a rape victim might list feelings of hurt, worthlessness, disgust in their prayer and not the fact that they were raped. The facts can never be changed, but the re-feelings (the resentments) can be healed. The clients are advised to post this prayer in an obvious place, such as on a bathroom mirror, so that they can be reminded by a daily activity, such as brushing teeth, to say the prayer.

It is in this step that the client makes the decision, daily, to access their internal spiritual power to help them heal. In making the simple choice to recite the prayer they have composed, the client decides to be spiritual, to be fully human. The story of Teigra shows how making such a decision can have dramatic results.

The Story of Teigra

Teigra was a senior in high school and she was, as her name implies, a tiger. She was raised in a home of alcoholics and as such had inculcated into her being their behaviors of emotional stoicism and emotional immaturity. She was also a rageaholic, having learned this from her dad, who drank himself to death when she was nine. Teigra knew only two kinds of sober emotional expression: the stone cold stare or an explosion of rage. Alcohol allowed her to experience different emotions and a feeling of closeness with her drinking friends, but the law saw her drinking differently. Teigra was frequently in trouble with the law. She had many MIPs, probation violations and assault and batteries. She had broken her stepfather's nose on several occasions. She had been placed in the teen home system, but nothing helped to calm the tiger. She was still tough and cold and had a tendency to explode in a rage of anger at the most inopportune time.

Teigra was court ordered to attend counseling. She was offered forgiveness therapy as a path to better emotional health, and she chose to work on forgiving her dad. She wrote the letter identifying her resentments towards him and then composed a prayer forgiving him for the hurt and anger she felt. It happened that soon after, Teigra was again jailed for another probation violation when she was caught drinking. This violation would probably result in 90 days in jail, which would prevent her from graduating on schedule. Teigra wanted desperately to belong, and graduating with her class would really feel good to her. Teigra related that the night before her court hearing, she prayed her prayer forgiving her dad "at least fifty thousand times." Teigra stated that something happened in court that had never happened before. She cried in court! The tiger had cried in court. Teigra went on to say that the judge seemed moved by this change in her behaviors and didn't give her jail time. Teigra considered it a miracle, as jail time was almost certain given all her previous charges. Teigra called it a miracle—and perhaps it was—but it was a self-imposed miracle, as she had made the decision to be spiritual and had thus broken through her emotional stoicism.

Teigra changed in other ways as well. Her self-assessment of her self-esteem increased from a two to a seven. She has learned how to get along in an alcoholic family system without resorting to violence. She graduated from high school and is now attending college.

Teigra changed dramatically in one night of praying. A lifetime of learned behaviors were circumvented when she was able to express her deeper emotions before the judge. That is the power available in the spiritual realm and can be accessed by prayer and forgiveness.

The second sentence of the prayer, "I ask God (or the client's chosen Higher Power) to forgive you also," was included due to the lesson learned from Ted's experience. Ted's inculcated childhood religious beliefs were of a vengeful God. Ted did pray that he would forgive his mother, but in his mind, he held out the possibility that his vengeful God would somehow pay his mother back for the hurt, shame and worthlessness he felt. For this reason, Ted was recommended to ask his Higher Power to forgive his mother as well. This would help to close the door that Ted kept open to his old resentments.

The wording of the prayer can be changed to suit the culture of the client. Even the word "prayer" has, in some situations, been replaced with the word "statement" if it is more culturally acceptable to the client. Jaba didn't pray a prayer of forgiveness; instead he meditated on a statement granting a reprieve to his dad. The effect was the same. The universal spiritual principle of forgiveness was used even though the words were different. The important point is to make the prayer or statement as individualized as possible to the client. The format given shouldn't be considered as a rigid tool but simply as a starting point from which to develop an individualized prayer. Most clients have never composed a prayer and are reluctant to do so even in the relative safety of the counseling office, which is why the format is used to start the process. The specific content of the prayer doesn't seem to matter a great deal as long as three necessary points are included; forgiveness, some of the major resentments and asking their Higher Power to forgive also. All of the resentments don't need to be listed because it appears that forgiveness becomes generalized to all of the resentments felt towards one person.

Make a separate prayer for each individual against whom there are resentments. Lumping together several people hasn't been tried. It has been suggested to some clients that they forgive whole cultures, but it has never actually been done on paper with this author. Whether or not these clients attempted to forgive a whole culture is not known. This area is ideal for further investigation into the appropriateness of forgiveness therapy.

What is prayer and what power does it have to heal? Dictionaries say that prayer is asking or entreating and in the second part of the prayer, it is obvious that there is asking forgiveness of a Higher Power. But prayer is more than just asking, it is a decision to access that realm of human experience called spiritual. Prayer might be more appropriately called "talking to." It is talking to the spiritual part of our being. This can be a new experience, this "talking to" our spiritual side. By making the decision to talk to our spiritual side, one is, in effect, admitting to the existence of the spiritual part of being. The next obvious question is what is the spiritual part of our being about? The answer is found in words like Love, caring, and forgiveness. These are spiritual concepts from the spiritual realm.

A distinction must be made here between spiritual and spiritism because it is spiritism that usually causes fear. Spiritism can be defined as interaction with spirits who exist at the lower or more negative end of the spiritual continuum. These spirits have been portrayed in movies and books as terrifying, fear-producing beings. There are few portrayals of loving, caring spirits, but not many. Spiritism is not the area where healing power is found, instead it is found in a different area called spirituality. Spirituality can be defined as the practice of universal spiritual principles, such as love, caring and empathy, in relationships with yourself, others and your Higher Power. It is accessing the positive, more powerful, side of the spiritual continuum. It is at this end of the spiritual realm where there is power to heal past resentments, as has been exhibited by many clients. Other phenomena can also be experienced in this realm, and that is the subject of the next chapter.

7

EPIPHANIES AND OTHER SPIRITUAL EXPERIENCES

A client choosing to use a spiritual approach to healing such as forgiveness therapy might have an experience that could be termed an epiphany, vision, white light experience, quantum change, moment of clarity or transformational experience. This subject area is discussed in more detail, in the book by William Miller and Janet C'de Baca called *Quantum Change: When Epiphanies and Sudden Insights Transform Ordinary Lives* (The Guilford Press, 2001). For the purposes of this book, the indicators of these types of experiences will be discussed so that a clinician can recognize what the client may have experienced and so that the symptoms aren't misdiagnosed as a mental health disorder.

A clinician that doesn't have much experience dealing with spiritual experiences may have the same fear that the client has when they first encounter this type of experience. This is fear generated from the unfamiliar. Harm could be done to the client if the clinician, out of his or her own fear, regresses to a strictly intellectual thought process and diagnoses a mental health disorder. These types of experiences can be powerful motivators if approached with the appropriate attitude. An attitude of open-mindedness, on the part of the clinician, will go a long way in helping the client to be transformed by the experience.

There are some common characteristics associated with people who have had these types of experiences. The first characteristic is that they often say that they don't have the words to describe it. They say the English language doesn't have the words or descriptors necessary to accurately portray their experience. Some people have resorted to metaphors or analogies as a way to describe the experience. Others have written songs or poems as a method to convey their thoughts and feelings and spirituality about the experience. When a client presents an inability to describe an event, it is possible that they have had some type of transformational experience.

The second characteristic commonly felt by recipients of visions, epiphanies and similar events is fear. They may express a fear of talking about what happened because they are afraid of being judged as crazy or being diagnosed with a mental health disorder. The *Diagnostic and Statistical Manual of Mental Disorders* (American Psychiatric Association, 2000), the prime reference for the field of psychology, makes no allowances for spiritual experiences and doesn't seem to even acknowledge this realm of human experiencing. But, it does list hearing voices or seeing visions as criteria for paranoid schizophrenia.

The client's fear needs to be explored in order to allow the power of the experience to work for positive change. They need to be supported psychologically and socially to help them to integrate the experience in their life. Help them to choose love and not fear by allowing them to talk about their experience without any judgment about their mental state. Do not reinforce, even subtly, any fears that they may express. Instead, try to convey an atmosphere of acceptance, curiosity, and inquisitiveness about how this experience can help them. The clinician is discouraged from pretending to understand. The nature of epiphanies through the ages has been that they contain a large element of mystery. The person having this type of experience will get continuing joy as parts of the mystery coalesce over time.

If a client is focusing on fear, it might be best to help them seek a loving and accepting stance to the experience. One way to do this is by using the following metaphor: portray the experience as a doorway to a new way of living. This new way of living has many unknowns. Not knowing or unfamiliarity can generate fear. Fear is expected in trying something new, but it shouldn't prevent the attempt. An example of using this doorway metaphor was a methamphetamine addict who claimed that God was with him in his car, saved his life and helped him to get home. He was very fearful of the experience and hadn't used for some weeks. His fear also motivated him to enter treatment, where he was seeking answers to this experience. His experience was reframed according to the doorway metaphor, where he could choose to walk through the door to a new way of life, a sober life. He was told that anything new usually has some fear associated with it. The doorway metaphor helped him to move through his fear and chose a life of sobriety. His attitude changed from one of fear to one of acceptance. Once the fear was removed, he then talked about the joy of the experience.

The choice between fear and love is fundamental in forgiveness therapy.

This choice is very similar to the choice to forgive or not to forgive. Both choices contrast the negative spiritual choice of fear against the positive spiritual choice, either love or forgiveness. People having transformational experiences are in a vulnerable state and at the same time are faced with stark choices to be made between fear and love. The vulnerability comes from the perceived lack of social acceptance of these types of experiences. The clinician can be the first accepting social contact and help to integrate the experience as a transforming power. Pathologizing the experience can have the opposite effect.

Joy is the third common characteristic to quantum change experiences. When asked if they have ever known joy before their epiphanies, some clients have said, "No, this is the first time I have experienced joy." Women have said that they knew joy at the birth of their children and that the joy of their epiphanies was equal to or greater than that joy.

The Story of Deedee

Deedee was a chronic alcoholic. She had been in and out of alcoholic treatment and psych wards numerous times in her adult life. Through her substantial counseling, Deedee had gained much awareness, admittance and acceptance of her resentments, yet she continued to hold on to major resentments against her father and her ex-husband. Deedee agreed to try Forgiveness Therapy and wrote a letter to her dad identifying her resentments. She then wrote a prayer forgiving him. She repeated the prayer daily until testing revealed that she had forgiven her father. She started to remember some positive and tender moments they had shared when she was a child.

Deedee was struggling mightily with her resentments towards her ex-husband. She would clench her fists in session and exclaim that she would never let go of these resentments. Tapping into this storehouse of pain and hurt was overwhelming and she would often resort to her old behavior of drinking to cope with this pain. She even tried suicide to cope with her feelings. Another side of Deedee wanted to be free of these resentments and would cry for some relief from the pain of her internal struggle. Deedee exhibited integrity: she would tell of those times when she would say her prayer forgiving her ex-husband and also those times when she wouldn't say the prayer. The times she said the prayer were very emotional for her because she had so much negative emotional energy stored up.

Deedee was developing a new concept of a Higher Power to replace her father. She was taught meditation techniques to help her in her communication with her new Higher Power.

In a following session, Deedee was strangely silent. When asked if everything was all right, Deedee said that she was afraid to talk about an experience she had because she thought she would be judged crazy. When reassured that this wouldn't happen and she would not be put in a psych ward, Deedee related the following experience but struggled to find the words to describe it. She said that she was at home alone and hadn't been drinking, and was trying the meditation techniques when something happened. Deedee said that she was in the presence of God and that she was in His presence for three hours! She said that during this time, she cried out all her hurt and pain that she had inside from her ex-husband. Deedee said that it was the most wondrous experience that she had ever had. She had never before experienced such Love, acceptance and joy. She finally let out all the tears and pain that she had been holding in for decades and decades.

Deedee's behaviors didn't change abruptly after this experience, but she is taking brave new steps in the direction of a sober life. She has a new goal, to live a life filled with the Love, joy and acceptance that she was able to know and experience in those three hours.

Deedee had all three characteristics of a person who has experienced an epiphany: she had fear about being judged as crazy, she had a hard time finding appropriate descriptor words, and she expressed joy. This experience has provided her a goal for the rest of her life. If it had been discounted in any way, she might not have benefited.

The Story of Shiloh

Shiloh was from a cultural minority where drug and alcohol addiction were more a way of life than a problem. To escape his own addictions would probably mean having to leave his culture, because the cultural influences to drink and use were more powerful than any tool a treatment program could provide. Still, Shiloh tried to work on his resentments that kept triggering him to use. His using had been partially connected to his inability to function socially with women when he was sober. A past girlfriend had hurt him deeply. He couldn't interact with any woman while sober and not be reminded of this pain. It took Shiloh some time to gain awareness, admittance and acceptance of his hurt. Writing a letter to his girlfriend telling how she had hurt him helped in the process. Shiloh then composed a prayer forgiving her for this hurt and consciously chose to say this prayer everyday until testing confirmed that he had forgiven her. Shiloh began to see results in that he could now talk to women freely even when sober. His bondage to his past hurts were gone.

Another benefit that Shiloh experienced was a vision. In Shiloh's vision, he saw what his future could be like if he were to stay away from drugs and alcohol. His vision would require a life of discipline, which is a foreign concept for an addict. Shiloh was fearful about the requirements to fulfill his vision, but at the same time he could sense a deep-seated joy at the prospect of making his vision come true.

Shiloh had two of the three characteristics of a transformational experience: joy and fear. He was also intrigued by the mystery of the experience. How could a drug addicted, minority person achieve the heights alluded to in his vision? It remains Shiloh's mystery to live out.

We have already heard the story of Jaba. He, too, had a vision where he saw his past, present, and a future filled with exhilarating hope. Jaba's vision brought him tears of joy. He experienced a joy that he had never known before, a joy that appeared to motivate him to come out of his darkness and live in the light. Jaba said that his vision and joy were a direct result of having granted his father a reprieve.

These types of experiences seem to be given to people who have chosen a spiritual path of healing through forgiveness therapy. Not all clients choosing this path have had these epiphanies; in fact, only a small percentage have talked about having a transformational experience. Nonetheless, they have happened, and when they do, it is wise practice to support and accept them, for in them may lie more positive energy for change than any therapist or counselor can possess, acquire or call into use.

8

FORGIVENESS TESTING

In developing this process, it became apparent that a method was needed to determine when a client was finished with an issue, if they had forgiven the person against whom they held resentments. Simply asking if they were done with the issue didn't seem to work because this intellectual question allowed them to remain in the mental realm, where their defenses resided. It was too easy for these defenses to guard their emotional truth.

As previously stated, Erik Skarstrom provided the method to get out of one's head and into the heart by placing the hand over the heart and speaking the feelings from under the hand. The test that was developed consists of having the client place their dominant hand over their heart, close their eyes, and state, "(insert name), I forgive you." The client is then asked to identify the feeling under their hand. If they can't identify the feeling, they are given a feelings list to help. To pass the forgiveness test, the client needs to repeat the test several times until he or she can identify two or three neutral or positive feelings in succession. It becomes obvious, after two or three repetitions, whether or not they have forgiven their abuser. Feelings of anger, hate, hurt, loneliness, abandonment, disgust, disgrace, worthlessness, fear or any other negative feelings indicate that they haven't finished forgiving. Three positive or neutral feelings in succession such as love, value, courage, comfort, peace, hope, pity or sadness indicate that they have finished with the resentment.

If a client is still answering from their defensive thought process, they will give flippant answers like, "I feel my heart beating." While this is true, it is an answer from the physical realm and not the emotional realm. It is also an indication of their unwillingness, at that time, to look deeper in themselves.

Kaspar's story is a good illustration of how forgiveness testing is used. Kaspar had three people against whom he held resentments. He chose to work on the least severe resentment first. He wrote the letter and then composed a prayer of forgiveness. He said the prayer daily for two weeks and was then tested. Kaspar's first two emotional responses were very mildly negative and then he gave three neutral responses in a row indicating that he had forgiven his abuser.

Kaspar then went on to work on forgiving the next most severe resentment by writing the letter to this abuser. While doing this exercise, he happened to be in the town where the abuse had occurred, and he realized that he had no more feelings of wanting to go and kill the abuser. It was postulated that perhaps Kaspar had already forgiven him by doing the letter, or that in forgiving his first abuser, something had been transferred to the current issue. The forgiveness test was put to use to see if he had forgiven this second abuser. Kaspar's test revealed that he had, in fact, forgiven the abuser even though he hadn't written the forgiveness prayer.

The test doesn't give any indication about how much work needs to be done on an issue—it only gives a yes or no answer about whether or not the resentment is finished with. But, as with Kaspar, it can be used as a benchmark so that valuable counseling time doesn't need to be spent on issues that are finished. Kaspar didn't need to write a prayer to his second abuser and spend time saying it daily because the forgiveness test indicated he was done with it. Kaspar never did mention this abuse incident again for the duration of his counseling, (about four months), whereas previous to this test, it was mentioned in almost every session. Kaspar had indicated earlier that he would kill this man if he could find him. During this time Kaspar was also suicidal, and one might question if these two issues are somehow linked. After Kaspar forgave this abuser, his urge to kill him went away and his suicidal ideation never returned.

The hand on the heart technique can be a very powerful experience the first time it is used because the person might be experiencing their true emotions, not protected by intellectual defenses, for the first time in their lives. Daisy had just such an experience. Daisy was working on forgiving her dad. In Daisy's perfect view of herself, she wasn't an angry person and had never allowed herself to feel true anger. Daisy didn't take the test on forgiving her father and chose not to continue working on it. Instead, she chose to work on forgiving God because she was angry at God for taking her father. (Working on forgiving God, for a person stuck in childhood trauma, is usually working on the father issue, just a little farther removed.) Daisy wrote a letter to God telling how she felt about Him taking her father. She then wrote a prayer forgiving God and after a few weeks of saying the prayer agreed to be tested. Daisy was willing to place her hand on her heart and be honest with herself about what she felt. Daisy consciously touched on her storehouse of anger for the first time in her life. She stayed with it long enough to see that underneath the anger, there was much pain and hurt. For the first time in her life, she consciously allowed herself to feel her true emotions without filtering them through her protective defenses. She was in awe of the whole experience. She made the connection that she wasn't mad at God, but at her father. She also saw for herself that under all this anger was a lot of hurt and pain.

Daisy was then willing to work on her resentment towards her dad. She started to say the prayer forgiving him and eventually tested as being finished with the resentment. Her step dad resentments were another issue. She wrote the letter identifying what her resentments are, but she is unwilling to forgive him; the time isn't right.

Before the test is administered, *the client is always asked if they want to be tested.* No time frame has ever been imposed. Instead, a person centered approach is used: it is presumed that the client will know when the time is right to be tested. Many clients, when asked if they were ready to be tested, answered no, not yet. They were then asked in following sessions if they were ready to be tested, and only when they indicated affirmatively were they tested. This is in keeping with the whole milieu of forgiveness therapy, where, because of the deep personal nature of this work, respect for the client's willingness to go forward is always the second consideration of the therapist. The first is to consider the safety of the client. First do no harm.

9

SAFETY AND PRECAUTIONS

Caution: the process outlined in this book can cause one to become suicidal! Take precautionary actions by having on hand emergency room phone numbers and crisis line phone numbers and resolve to use them if you start to think about suicide or harming yourself in any way. **Have these numbers ready before you start the process!**

There is risk involved in any counseling or therapeutic process. That risk comes from looking at emotionally charged issues. Forgiveness therapy can open up these emotionally charged issues at the deepest levels, and one needs to be prepared to cope with these emotions. The emotions of feeling hopeless, helpless and worthless are three that can be the precursors of suicidal thoughts. If you find yourself feeling any of these emotions or having thoughts of harming yourself in any way, seek help immediately! Talk to somebody. Call a crisis line, 911 or an emergency room.

The risks of this process were brought to light by a client we will call Ivan. Ivan had been abused by both of his drug-addicted parents for several years when he was young. The more obvious abuse of repeated rapes and beatings were compounded by his lack of emotional learning, which prevented Ivan from identifying or expressing how he felt about his abuse—or any emotions, for that matter. Ivan had received considerable counseling during his stays in juvenile detention facilities and jails, but he still struggled with identifying and expressing his emotions. It took some time for him to develop a measure of emotional maturity and after he did, he indicated that he was willing to try to forgive his parents.

Ivan presented as a real tough guy. He was a product of the streets and jails. He could handle anything, even forgiving his parents. He hadn't had any history of suicidal thoughts or attempts, but he was given crisis line numbers as a safety precaution when starting the process of forgiveness. Ivan wrote a letter to his father and started to remember more abuse than he could stand to feel. He felt worthless. He found himself sitting on his basement floor with the means to end his life. He didn't; instead, he called the crisis line. He reached out for help. He then called other people who care for him. He talked about his near suicide in his next counseling session and he also composed a prayer forgiving his father in this session. Ivan said it may take time to forgive his dad, but he is trying.

Ivan had kept his feelings at a distance with many addictions. When he took an in-depth honest look at his resentments for the first time, it was almost too much for him to bear, but he did the right thing by reaching out for help. He could have turned to chemicals to numb his pain — and he considered it — but he chose to trust another human to share his pain. Nobody, not even Ivan, knew the depth of pain and hurt that was inside. Ivan's willingness to do the spiritual work of trying to heal opened up the whole depth of his pain. This is the risk of doing this kind of work.

Deedee was another client who became suicidal during the process of forgiving. Deedee had a history of suicidal attempts. She, too, was given the crisis line numbers to contact in case of suicidal ideation. She also had daily visits by home health care workers, but this didn't prevent her from attempting suicide again. Deedee tried to kill herself by taking all the pills in her house and then drinking as much as she could. A home health care worker found her and called 911. Deedee didn't reach out for help and it was only because of her home health care worker that she lived.

Exactly how much of Deedee's suicidal attempt is due to her working on forgiving her ex-husband will never be known, especially taking into account her previous attempts at suicide, but her case illustrates the need for precautions.

Deedee's and Ivan's cases both indicate that although forgiveness is a path of healing freely chosen, it can still lead to emotions that are difficult to deal with. These difficult emotions, when not dealt with, are a large contributing factor in the continuance of their addictions. Both Deedee and Ivan had copious amounts of counseling which hadn't done anything to remove their resentments or their addictions. Both of them were willing to try forgiveness therapy and were informed of the risks before starting.

Therapists or counselors who choose to use this therapy are advised to talk about the risks with their clients before the client makes their freewill choice to proceed or not. Letter-writing assignments are given out in a preprinted format so that emergency numbers can be written on the same page. For higher risk clients, it might be better practice to also give out a business card-sized paper with emergency contact numbers on it, to keep in their purse or wallet. It would also be wise practice to look for signs of suicidal tendencies when a client is involved in this process. At every session, ask about their feelings, and be on the lookout for feelings of worthlessness, hopelessness and helplessness. If a client is expressing any of these feelings or any suicidal ideation, plan, or means—take the appropriate measures to ensure the safety of the client.

This is deep therapy in the spiritual realm and the emotions that are exposed can be very intense. A client's willingness to try a spiritual solution is inclusive of an honest look at the problem. Most cases involve intense resentments—so intense that they may have never looked at them before and kept them buried by using drugs and alcohol. In offering forgiveness therapy as a healing path, one is offering the hope of healing these wounds. It is this hope that allows the clients to look deeply into themselves. This deep introspection reveals the buried hurt and pain. However, this buried hurt and pain is also the source of the risk. Is this risk worth the return? That is for the client to decide and is one reason why forgiveness therapy must be a freewill choice.

10

CLINICAL EVIDENCE OF FORGIVENESS

There can be other evidence, in addition to having passed the forgiveness test, that the issue has been worked through. Deedee, for example, passed the forgiveness test on the issue with her father and she also started to remember some positive things from her past childhood with him. She remembered a special Christmas present that he had gotten her, and this brought tears of joy to her eyes some sixty odd years later. She also remembered how he used to play his banjo on the porch and how happy this used to make her feel. These good feelings had been blocked by Deedee's resentments towards her dad. After these resentments were healed, by forgiving him, she then had access to the positive memories of her dad. This balanced view, seeing both the good and the evil, is evidence that the issue with her dad was resolved. Another sign of her healing was that she no longer spoke of her resentments in session, whereas previous to her forgiving him, she spoke of this issue in almost every session. Deedee also stopped asking why her father had abused her.

Abe had many symptoms that disappeared soon after he forgave his dad. His poor performance in school improved. His sleep problems and nightmares went away. His anxiety levels went down. He doesn't have the recurring thoughts of needing to stay busy all the time. His backlog of anger is gone. His relationships with family and friends are better. All this is clinical evidence of his improved functioning and is a direct benefit of his willingness to forgive his dad.

Jaba demonstrated clinical improvement in that his attitude on life was much healthier. Prior to granting his father a reprieve, he had stated that he liked to live his life in the dark, literally and figuratively. He was expressing no hope for his future and looked at life as an endurance and acceptance of fear. After going through the process, he gained hope and began to set goals, and took concrete actions toward achieving them. Jaba's change could be classed as a third order change because his outlook on the world as a place of fear was changed to an outlook of hope and freedom. His original world view had been transformed to a completely different world view.

Grace's changed outlook could also be viewed as a third order change. She used to view the world as a place to escape from with drugs and alcohol. After forgiving her abusers, she started to have hope for a better future. She could see the possibilities inside and outside herself. She began to trust people. Will Grace have an idyllic life? Probably not, but she has a good chance at leading a normal life now that she isn't encumbered with all of the negative influences from her past.

Cameo didn't exhibit a radical change in her outlook on life, but she is functioning better. Her self-esteem is higher and she is able to make and defend appropriate boundaries. Before going through this process, Cameo was easily taken advantage of by people in her life. Her employer would ask her to do things that were not part of her job, which would take away from her time with her family. She couldn't stand up to this employer, but after going through forgiveness therapy, she was able to stand up for her rights.

One of Shiloh's problems was that he couldn't be with a girl without being high because he would be reminded of the pain from a previous relationship. After forgiving this woman, he was able to talk and be with a woman without the assistance of drugs. Again, this is clinical evidence of improved functioning. Shiloh may have experienced a third order change depending on how he makes use of his vision. If he makes an effort to discipline himself to the requirements of his vision, then there will be a third order change. If he doesn't discipline himself the change will be of a lesser order or no change at all. There is also the possibility that if Shiloh turns away from his vision, he will be turning to a more destructive life than he knew before.

Kaspar had many clinical improvements over the course of his forgiveness therapy. His homicidal and suicidal ideation went away. He returned to work. He started a new and healthier relationship than those he had before. He gained hope and goals for his future and started to work on achieving his goals by starting college. He resumed interest in his hobbies. Kaspar's change was a third order change because he went from suicidal ideation to enjoying life.

These examples of improved clinical functioning have been repeated many times. Most clients, having gone through this process of forgiveness, related that their lives have improved dramatically. They express feelings of joy, freedom, hope, higher self-esteem and a whole plethora of improved feelings. Another significant clinical improvement that was observed in most clients completing Forgiveness Therapy `was long term (more than one year) continued sobriety.

Were resentments viewed or treated as the only cause of addiction? No. Most of the clients mentioned also received other forms of substance abuse counseling. Resentments were viewed as a block to long-term sobriety, and if this block wasn't removed the chances for continued sobriety decreased.

At the beginning of the development of this process, it was apparent that some other measure of effectiveness would be helpful in addition to the forgiveness test. The public system of treatment for substance abuse is basically a behavior-oriented system, and as such, requires a measurement of the success or failure of any method. The question was how to measure the success of a humanistic/spiritual method. The tool that proved useful was a Likert Scale self-assessment of self-esteem. Clients agreeing to participate in forgiveness therapy were asked what they felt their self-esteem was on a scale of one to ten, with ten being the highest and one the lowest. The question was asked again after they had finished working on their resentments with forgiveness therapy. The majority of cases assessed their self-esteem as significantly higher after participating in forgiveness therapy.

There was one client that was prominent during this development period, because at first it looked forgiveness therapy had made his life worse. This client agreed to try forgiveness therapy as a possible method of ending his chronic, long-term alcoholism. He had a history of abuse similar to other clients. He also had co-occurring mental health disorders, not unlike some of the other clients who were successful. He struggled with the letter-writing (as had other clients). He did compose a prayer, but related that he was unwilling to recite his prayer daily. Any reminders of his pain would send him back to the bottle. His drinking became much worse and he left counseling. His life spiraled back down into the pit where he was alone in his pain and he refused help from anyone. In later contacts with this client, he related that he eventually did spend a considerable amount of time reciting his prayer and that he had gained a measure of peace and serenity concerning his abuse issues.

Like any therapy, there will be successes and cases that appear to be failures but are merely slow changers. With forgiveness therapy, there seems to be more successes. This hasn't been scientifically validated, but has been intuitively validated. Any scientist willing to put together a study to gain scientific validation is welcome to do so.

11

COST EFFECTIVENESS

The question about the cost effectiveness of forgiveness therapy came up in a staff meeting where the case of Kana was being discussed.

The Story of Kana

Kana was in trouble with the law. He had received a minor in possession charge and had been repeatedly violated on probation for the use of marijuana. Kana had a problem with his self-esteem; he didn't have any. When asked to evaluate his self-esteem on a scale from one to ten, he said it was zero. His bodily scars testified to this fact. His arms were covered with burn circles where he had pushed lit cigarettes against his skin. His wrists and forearms had many small scars from his cutting behaviors. Some of the cuts were fresh and scabbed over. The knuckles and fingers of Kana's hands resembled those of a much older man who had done hard labor. Kana, however, was only 19. The rough condition of his hands bespoke the many times he had struck out in raging anger at brick walls and telephone poles, breaking his fingers and knuckles.

In the very first counseling session, where Kana indicated his lack of self-esteem, he stated that it would be great if he could raise his self-esteem to a one. He said that he couldn't feel good about himself because he didn't know who he was. Kana would apologize profusely for any little slight he thought he may have caused. If he was five minutes late, he would apologize three times.

Kana's assessment revealed the root cause of his condition to be a set of circumstances over which he had no control, but for which he was made responsible at an early age. Kana's father had been killed when Kana was five years old. Kana's alcoholic family system unknowingly deprived him of the grieving process. A short time after his father's death, Kana's mother hooked up with another man. This man brought with him several daughters.

These new additions brought something else into Kana's young life, a dysfunction where they blamed Kana for all the problems of this blended family. They even told young Kana that he was responsible for his father's death! Kana's mother didn't intervene to protect her young son. The abuse by his step dad and step sisters continued for years and eventually even mom started to blame Kana for all of her problems.

Kana revealed that he held much anger for his father, who had left him in this situation and wasn't there to protect him. These resentments crowded out any logical thought process, which would have allowed an objective determination of, "How could I, a five year old child, have been responsible for my father's death?"

Kana's family system provided no validation of who Kana was other than the family scapegoat. His defined role in the family was forced upon him from the time his step dad and step sisters moved in with their dysfunctional baggage and unloaded it on young Kana.

Kana's dreams gave evidence of where he was stuck. Kana spoke of a dream that came often to haunt his nights. He dreamt of walking down a road and sitting beside this road was a figure in a long black robe that covered his head. As he walked by this specter, it would slowly pull the robe down exposing his head. It was Kana's father, but something was terribly wrong. Part of his skull was missing and there were other gross injuries to his head. It was at this point that Kana would awaken from his dream in a panic. He initially tried to seek solace from his mom when these dreams happened, but she rebuffed him.

Kana also dreamt of standing in front of his dad's casket. In this dream, Kana saw gross deformities in the head and face of his father. Kana related that he was never crying in this dream; instead, he was frozen in a state of fear and unable to move. Kana's emotions were also frozen.

Kana was offered the path of forgiveness as a way to free himself from the past. He accepted and started down the path with the warning that this might be the most difficult thing he had ever attempted. It was recommended that Kana work on a resentment of less magnitude first to gain comfort and trust in the process. Kana refused this recommendation and stated that he wanted to work on his resentments towards his father first because they were the ones giving him the most problems.

Kana had difficulty writing the letter to his dad, but with help, he was able to complete the letter-writing assignment. The resentments that Kana identified were that he felt abandoned, unprotected and unloved. He was also able to remember some positive things about his dad. Kana then composed a prayer forgiving his dad and asking his Higher Power to forgive his dad also. Kana stated that it was his intention to repeat this prayer daily, and he did. In three weeks of saying his prayer daily, Kana changed dramatically. His emotions started to move. He was no longer stuck. He could cry freely. He became open to learning assertiveness techniques. He completed a visualization exercise where he went and found his young self, standing in front of his dad's casket and cried with him there. Kana then visualized gently taking his young self from that place of horrors and bringing him to a safe place. The nightmares stopped. Kana's self-esteem rose abruptly. He now assessed his self-esteem as a five. He stopped all self-mutilating behaviors. Kana stood up to the continuing abuse by his step dad and commanded that it stop. It did. Kana related that his drug use had mostly stopped and that his changed attitude was being noticed at his work. Kana began to develop some goals and a hope for his future. He was no longer a slave to his past.

Kana's miraculous turnaround happened over a span of approximately two months of weekly one-hour sessions. The main therapeutic tool was Kana's own willingness to try to forgive his dad.

Kana's case was discussed in a staff meeting. The subject was the economic efficiency of his recovery. The counselors present agreed that if Kana can maintain his gains over the course of his life, it would be worth at least $500,000. This figure was arrived at by including decreased medical and psychological costs and increased earning potential. The direct costs of Kana's counseling were about $500. This would yield a very impressive return on investment of about 1000 to 1. Forgiveness therapy is, indeed a cost effective method of healing.

Other stories in this book have also demonstrated the cost effectiveness of forgiveness therapy. Abe, for example, had years of counseling and therapy to address an identified problem. His working through a process of forgiveness cured his problems in a matter of weeks. Again, the cost effectiveness is very obvious.

Jaba had been in the system for many years and had consumed thousands of public treatment dollars. His life was in a stall and he could have easily gone back into the system, but he chose to grant a reprieve to his dad, thereby freeing Jaba from his past. This freedom also included being free from public treatment or incarceration dollars. Jaba said, "This was the best counseling I have ever gotten."

Grace had been a dependent of the state for many years. She had counseling and therapy, but her life wasn't getting much better. After forgiving her abusers, her life started to get better. She was becoming less dependent on the system because she had found the power, inside, to take care of herself. That power will be a huge preventative factor in keeping her from a life of drugs and incarceration.

Many clients have had large amounts of public money spent on the hope of their recovery, and while money is power, there is inside all humans a power to heal that is greater than money. This power to heal is spiritual and can be accessed through forgiveness therapy.

It would seem wise for the budget decision-makers in the mental health care industry to investigate the cost effectiveness and the return on investment that is possible with forgiveness therapy.

12

HELPING YOURSELF

Can you use this process of forgiveness to help yourself? Yes, you can, but you need to take some safety precautions. First, you need to get the phone numbers of crisis lines, emergency rooms or other mental health agencies in your area. Include 911 on your list of numbers if it is available in your area. Write these phone numbers down on a business card and carry it with you until you are done with this process. Also, you must have the resolve to use these phone numbers if you start to have any thoughts about harming yourself in any way.

Forgiveness therapy is extremely deep work. You may not even know what is down there and you need to be prepared to deal with anything. If you have doubts about your ability to handle intense emotions like feeling worthless, helpless, hopeless and you still want to try to work through your resentments with forgiveness therapy, bring this book to a professional mental health care counselor or therapist, and ask them to help you work the process. Another reason to seek professional help is that the therapist is trained to look for signs of problems before they become acute. If you can't ask people you know to help you, for whatever reason, then a therapist can provide a confidential trusting relationship to help you work trough your resentments.

In seeking professional help, you are not looking for healing power in the therapist; that power resides in you. Instead, you are looking for someone to help you to insure your safety and someone to listen to your emotions. Resentments are emotional pain that we keep re-feeling or that we try to keep from re-feeling. A trained professional can help you to deal with this emotional pain in a safe manner.

If you are going to proceed without professional help, some emotional intelligence is needed. There are feelings lists in Appendix 4 of this book and it is recommended that you copy them and use them to help you to identify your feelings. This can be a simple exercise of taking some time each day and circle on the list the feelings you have experienced that day.

The next step in gaining some emotional intelligence is to express the feelings that you have identified on the list to a caring person. This might be harder than it seems if you live in a system that is itself emotionally immature. To test your environment for emotional maturity or intelligence, go to a person and ask them to listen to your feelings. Use a very rigid formula and say, "I feel (insert a feeling word from the list)." Pay attention to their response. Do they listen attentively or do they make statements like, "You shouldn't feel that way" or some other statement that aims to change the way you feel? If they respond in this manner, you live in an emotionally immature system. Find somebody who is emotionally mature to listen to your feelings.

Feelings are emotional energy that indicate to us how our life is going. The only healthy thing that we can do with this emotional energy is to express it. Expressing this energy can take many forms, such as if we feel angry, we could exercise to exert this energy. Another way to express our feelings is to tell them to someone who cares. If this energy isn't expressed, it becomes stuck within us. This stuck emotional energy becomes a resentment.

If you would like a fast method to identify your true emotions, put your dominant hand, the right hand for right-handed people and the left hand for left-handed people, on your heart and comprehend the feeling under your hand. This method takes one out of their defenses, which live in their head. If this is difficult, it may be because you are still trying to answer the question "Why?" This means you are looking for healing in the intellectual realm. There is no healing power for resentments in the intellectual realm. You are trying to seek understanding as a path to healing, but you are trying to understand insanity. You are looking for light where there is only darkness. A better choice would be to seek healing in the spiritual realm, where there is healing power and light. Choosing to forgive is choosing a lighted path to healing power. Choosing a spiritual path may be a new experience to you, and may generate some fear. Courage is the antidote to this fear and one does need courage to try a spiritual path of forgiveness. This fear may have been greatly exaggerated by the experiences of your life, where the spiritual realm is usually portrayed in movies and books as a very negative and fearful place. Your religion may also have contributed to your fear of the spiritual. In reality, spirituality can simply be a consciousness of universal spiritual principles like love, caring, empathy and forgiveness.

After you have taken care of the safety measures, gained some emotional maturity, and are cognizant of your fear of the spiritual and have the courage to work through it, you are ready to proceed with the methods outlined in this book. First, you need to have some awareness of what resentments you are going to work on. If you have suffered some blatant form of abuse, it becomes a matter of identifying, with the aid of feelings lists, those feelings you keep re-feeling. If, on the other hand, you have resentments and can't get a clear picture of where they came from, you are going to have to do some more searching. To aid in that search, some examples will be discussed of abuse that isn't so obvious.

Neglect is often a difficult form of abuse to see, especially if it has a socially acceptable covering over it. An example of this is where parents are more concerned about their outward appearance, their facade, than they are about the care of their children. To everybody except their children, they appear to have model lives. They may be leaders in business, education or religion and show an outward appearance of having their lives together. When you talk to their children, however, they have a totally different story to tell. The children tell of parents who don't care for them beyond the surface appearance. These children often can't tell how they were abused, but they know they have resentments. There is an internal struggle between surface appearances and what they felt. There is parental hypocrisy that is hard to put into words. Outwardly, the family looked fine, even exemplary, but underneath the polished exterior, something is wrong. The basic problem is that the parents didn't know how to love. They knew how to look good for the public, but that is not love. This, then, becomes a difficult abuse to identify when the child, or grown child, wants to be free of this negative parental influence. The social structure probably supports the denial of this abuse because from the outside, the family was "normal" or "better than normal." This abuse by the parents wasn't an overt act, but an omission of caring acts. Another way to view this is to look at the parental priorities. Did they give attention to other people or principles and exclude the needs of their children? These principles or people could be their own selfishness, their job, their addiction(s), their fear(s), their money, their religion or their new partner in cases of divorce or death of a spouse. The resentments originating from this type of abuse can include a feeling of being unloved, worthless, shame and abandonment, but don't limit yourself to this list. Instead, use the feelings list to identify your own resentments/feelings. Be reassured that many people have these types of resentments towards their parents. Don't judge yourself as being right or wrong for having them. They just are, and are issues that can be healed with forgiveness therapy.

A test that you can use to check for resentments is to ask yourself the following question. Did I feel loved by this person, who could by their very position, be expected to love me? If the answer is no, then there are probably resentments present.

The identification of what needs to be forgiven can be a difficult obstacle to overcome, but if you are willing to remain open-minded and be honest about what your feelings are, then the resentments become much clearer. You might want to get outside objective help in identifying your resentments. This help might come from professionals, friends, books, talk shows or other family members who may be trying to heal from the same abuse. Rarely will the perpetrators of the hurt and pain be willing to help in this process; they have their energy invested in denial.

Once we have awareness of what has happened to us, we proceed to the difficult process of admitting to ourselves that we were somehow abused or neglected. This can be a double whammy effect of having to admit to being abused and also admitting that perhaps the person, who was supposed to love us, not only didn't, but abused us as well. This difficult step is giving up our childhood fantasies and expectations of perfect, loving, caring parents. It may be easier, in the short run, to live in denial or fantasy. We could use excuses that it wasn't abuse or that everybody did that back then, but this is invalidating our true emotions and supporting the denial. But somewhere in us, there are the feelings that something wasn't right. These are the resentments. They are feelings that can't be denied forever. Now is the time to write the letter. The letter format is found in Appendix 1.

The letter starts with some good things that this person may have done for you and is included to start the acceptance phase, from which a more balanced view of the person can be obtained. If no good things can be remembered at this point, it is alright to leave this part of the format blank. It may be that your resentments are so large that they block any good remembrances.

If the abuse issue you are working on is abuse by a stranger or by someone with whom you have had very little social interaction, such as being raped by a stranger, leave the first portion of the letter format blank. There are no expectations that there be any good remembrances from this type of situation.

Now, look deep inside. Allow yourself to feel the anger, the hurt and the pain. Use the feelings list and write down your feelings. Admit, maybe for the first time, your feelings about being abused and write them down to help get them out. Then put the letter away for some time. Give yourself time to accept your situation and your resentments. When you are ready, make the decision to forgive and formalize it by composing a prayer of forgiveness using the format from Appendix 3.

In composing the prayer, keep it short and simple because you are going to say it daily. All the issues don't need to be listed because forgiveness can be generalized, which means that forgiving a person for a couple of issues results in forgiveness for all of the hurts they have done to you. So, just list the major resentments.

Repeat the prayer daily, no matter what you are feeling. Choosing a spiritual path is choosing spirituality over emotion. The two are different and your emotions need not control your decision to be spiritual. It can be difficult work to choose to be forgiving when your emotions are anger, hatred, pain or hurt. But this is exactly the problem with resentments-to stay in the intellectual and emotional realm is to have justification for your feelings. Your feelings are right and justified in the intellectual/emotional realm. To heal, you need to make the decision to be spiritual, to forgive. When you have finished forgiving, the good feelings will come. It is a matter of trusting in the process and the testimonials of the clients in this book who have gone through the process and now have the good feelings. Keep repeating the prayer daily until, by an honest appraisal of your feelings, use the forgiveness test and the hand on the heart technique, you know you are finished with this resentment.

Can you make an honest appraisal of your feelings? Another method to help with getting to your true emotions is to stand in front of a mirror, place your hand on your heart, and say, "I forgive (insert name) for (insert resentment)." Look into your eyes and state the feeling under your hand. If you can do this two or three times, with a neutral or positive feeling, then you have successfully forgiven this person. Congratulations, you are free from this bondage. You can continue to work the process for any other resentments you may have.

Picking Them Up Again

You have freely chosen to forgive someone and are free from this bondage, but you can choose to go back into slavery. All it takes is picking up your old resentments. This can be avoided by using an emotion-stopping process where you refute your emotional thinking by making a statement like, "NO, I have forgiven that person." In doing so, you are choosing to access positive spiritual energy instead of giving in to negative power in the mental – emotional realm. The memory of the resentments will probably always be in this realm because human beings are memory beings, but the emotional power of the memory will fade. We are also spiritual beings and as such can choose to access this realm by simply saying to yourself that, "I have forgiven them."

APPENDIX 1
Letter Format

Emergency Numbers: _____

_____

Dear (   ), this is what you gave me that I am thankful for...

This is what you did to me, and this is how I feel....

This page can be reproduced without permission.

APPENDIX 2
Alternate Letter Format

Emergency Numbers: _____

_____

Dear (   ), this is what you gave me that I am thankful for...

This is what you didn't give me, and this is how I feel....

This page can be reproduced without permission.

APPENDIX 3
Prayer Format

Emergency Numbers: _____

_____

(   ), I forgive you for...

I ask_____ to forgive you also.

This page can be reproduced without permission.

APPENDIX 4
Feelings List

Abandoned
Abused
Accepted
Admired
Afraid
Alienated
Alive
Angry
Annoyed
Antagonistic
Anxious
Apathetic
Apprehensive
Awed
Bad
Bashful
Bitter
Bored
Brave
Capable
Caring
Cared-for
Cheated
Concerned
Confident
Confused
Courage
Courageous
Defeated
Defiant
Degraded
Dejected
Dependent
Depressed
Despised
Devalued

Disappointed
Disgusted
Disturbed
Down
Embarrassed
Empathy
Empty
Envious
Esteemed
Excited
Exhausted
Exploited
Fatigued
Fear
Fed-up
Free
Frozen
Frightened
Frustrated
Glad
Grateful
Gratified
Guilty
Happy
Hate
Helpless
Hopeful
Hopeless
Horrified
Humble
Humiliated
Hurt
Impatient
Important
Impotent
Inadequate

Independent
Indifferent
Inferior
Inspired
Joyful
Liked
Listless
Lonely
Loved
Mad
Miserable
Mixed-up
Moody
Nervous
Pain
Panicky
Passionate
Patient
Peaceful
Pleased
Proud
Provoked
Puzzled
Regretful
Rejected
Relieved
Reluctant
Respected
Resentful
Sad
Scared
Secure
Self-conscious
Self-pity
Shame
Shocked

Shy
Sick
Smothered
Strong
Stuck
Submissive
Sullen
Suspicious
Sympathetic
Tender
Tense
Terrified
Terrorized
Thankful
Threatened
Torn-up
Trapped
Troubled
Trusting
Uncomfortable
Unhappy
Unimportant
Unloved
Unpopular
Unsure
Upset
Used
Useless
Vengeful
Violated
Wanted
Weak
Worn-out
Worried
Worthless
Worthy

This page can be reproduced without permission.